The Retailer's Guide to Supply Chain Analytics and Optimization

Davis Ann

Copyright © [2023]

Title: The Retailer's Guide to Supply Chain Analytics and Optimization

Author's: Davis Ann

All rights reserved. No part of this publication may be reproduced, stored in a retrieval system, or transmitted in any form or by any means, electronic, mechanical, photocopying, recording, or otherwise, without the prior written permission of the publisher or author, except in the case of brief quotations embodied in critical reviews and certain other non-commercial uses permitted by copyright law.

This book was printed and published by [Publisher's: **Davis Ann**] in [2023]

ISBN:

TABLE OF CONTENT

Chapter 1: Introduction to Supply Chain Analytics — 07

Understanding the Importance of Supply Chain Analytics in Retail

Overview of Supply Chain Optimization Techniques

Benefits of Implementing Supply Chain Analytics in Retail

Challenges in Adopting Supply Chain Analytics in Retail

Chapter 2: Key Concepts in Supply Chain Analytics — 17

Defining Supply Chain Analytics

Types of Data Used in Supply Chain Analytics

Key Performance Indicators in Retail Supply Chains

Predictive Analytics in Retail Supply Chains

Chapter 3: Data Collection and Management for Supply Chain Analytics   26

Collecting Relevant Data for Supply Chain Analytics

Data Quality and Validation Techniques

Data Storage and Retrieval Methods

Data Security and Privacy Concerns in Retail Supply Chains

Chapter 4: Analytical Techniques for Supply Chain Optimization   34

Descriptive Analytics in Retail Supply Chains

Diagnostic Analytics for Identifying Supply Chain Issues

Predictive Analytics for Demand Forecasting

Prescriptive Analytics for Optimal Decision Making

Chapter 5: Implementing Supply Chain Analytics in Retail   43

Steps to Successful Implementation of Supply Chain Analytics

Building an Analytics Team in Retail Organizations

Selecting and Implementing Analytical Tools and Technologies

Integrating Supply Chain Analytics with Existing Systems

Chapter 6: Case Studies in Retail Supply Chain Analytics　　　　52

Case Study 1: Optimizing Inventory Management with Analytics

Case Study 2: Improving Supply Chain Efficiency through Predictive Analytics

Case Study 3: Enhancing Customer Satisfaction with Prescriptive Analytics

Case Study 4: Overcoming Challenges in Implementing Supply Chain Analytics

Chapter 7: Future Trends in Supply Chain Analytics for Retailers　　　　62

Emerging Technologies in Supply Chain Analytics

Artificial Intelligence and Machine Learning in Retail Supply Chains

Big Data Analytics and its Impact on Retail Supply Chains

Predictive Analytics for Omni-channel Retailing

Chapter 8: Conclusion and Recommendations   71

Summary of Key Findings

Recommendations for Retailers Implementing Supply Chain Analytics

Future Outlook for Supply Chain Analytics in Retail

Chapter 1: Introduction to Supply Chain Analytics

Understanding the Importance of Supply Chain Analytics in Retail

In today's rapidly evolving retail landscape, it has become increasingly crucial for retailers to leverage the power of data and analytics to optimize their supply chain operations. This subchapter aims to shed light on the immense importance of supply chain analytics in the retail industry, specifically targeting retailers and business standard analysts.

Supply chain analytics refers to the process of collecting, analyzing, and interpreting data related to the various aspects of the supply chain, with the ultimate goal of enhancing efficiency, reducing costs, and improving customer satisfaction. This analytical approach enables retailers to gain valuable insights into their supply chain operations, helping them make informed decisions and drive business growth.

One of the key benefits of supply chain analytics in retail is its ability to identify and mitigate potential risks and disruptions. By analyzing historical data and utilizing predictive modeling techniques, retailers can anticipate potential bottlenecks and proactively implement strategies to minimize their impact. This enables retailers to optimize inventory levels, reduce stockouts, and ensure seamless product availability, ultimately enhancing customer satisfaction and loyalty.

Furthermore, supply chain analytics empowers retailers to optimize their logistics and distribution networks. By analyzing data related to transportation costs, delivery times, and inventory levels, retailers can identify areas of improvement and make data-driven decisions to streamline their supply chain operations. This not only reduces costs but also improves overall operational efficiency, enabling retailers to deliver products to customers faster and at a lower cost.

Moreover, supply chain analytics plays a pivotal role in demand forecasting and inventory management. By analyzing historical sales data, market trends, and customer behavior, retailers can accurately predict future demand patterns and adjust their inventory levels accordingly. This ensures that retailers maintain optimal stock levels, minimizing the risk of overstocking or stockouts. Additionally, by leveraging analytics, retailers can identify slow-moving products, optimize pricing strategies, and improve product assortment to maximize profitability.

In conclusion, supply chain analytics has become an indispensable tool for retailers in today's competitive business landscape. By harnessing the power of data and analytics, retailers can optimize their supply chain operations, reduce costs, enhance customer satisfaction, and drive business growth. Business standard analysts should prioritize understanding and implementing supply chain analytics to unlock its vast potential for retailers in various niches.

Overview of Supply Chain Optimization Techniques

In today's rapidly evolving retail landscape, optimizing the supply chain has become crucial for retailers to gain a competitive edge. Supply chain optimization refers to the process of maximizing efficiency and minimizing costs throughout the entire supply chain, from sourcing raw materials to delivering the final product to customers. This subchapter aims to provide retailers, especially business standard analysts, with an overview of the various techniques available for supply chain optimization.

1. Demand Forecasting: Accurate demand forecasting is the foundation of a well-optimized supply chain. By leveraging historical data, market trends, and customer insights, retailers can predict demand patterns and make informed decisions regarding production, inventory, and distribution.

2. Inventory Management: Effective inventory management ensures that retailers have the right products in the right quantities at the right time. Techniques such as ABC analysis, economic order quantity (EOQ), and just-in-time (JIT) inventory help minimize holding costs, prevent stockouts, and streamline replenishment processes.

3. Transportation Optimization: Efficient transportation is vital for timely delivery and cost savings. Retailers can employ techniques like route optimization, load consolidation, and mode selection to minimize transportation costs, reduce delivery lead times, and enhance customer satisfaction.

4. Supplier Collaboration: Collaborating closely with suppliers can lead to improved supply chain performance. Techniques like vendor-

managed inventory (VMI), collaborative planning, forecasting, and replenishment (CPFR), and electronic data interchange (EDI) facilitate seamless communication, shared visibility, and effective coordination between retailers and suppliers.

5. Warehouse Optimization: Optimizing warehouse operations is essential for minimizing order processing time, reducing labor costs, and improving overall efficiency. Retailers can utilize techniques like slotting optimization, cross-docking, and automated storage and retrieval systems (AS/RS) to streamline warehouse layouts, maximize space utilization, and enhance order fulfillment speed.

6. Data Analytics and Technology: Leveraging advanced analytics and technology solutions can unlock valuable insights and enable real-time decision-making in supply chain optimization. Retailers can utilize tools like artificial intelligence (AI), machine learning (ML), and predictive analytics to identify patterns, optimize processes, and respond quickly to changes in demand or supply.

By implementing these supply chain optimization techniques, retailers can achieve numerous benefits, including reduced costs, improved customer service levels, increased operational efficiency, and enhanced profitability. However, it is important to note that each retailer's supply chain is unique, and a tailored approach is necessary to select and implement the most suitable techniques based on specific business requirements.

In conclusion, supply chain optimization plays a pivotal role in the success of retailers. This subchapter has provided an overview of the key techniques available for supply chain optimization, catering to the needs of business standard analysts in the retail industry. By employing these techniques, retailers can ensure a streamlined supply chain, gain a competitive advantage, and meet the ever-changing demands of their customers in today's dynamic retail landscape.

Benefits of Implementing Supply Chain Analytics in Retail

In today's highly competitive retail industry, staying ahead of the curve is critical for success. One way retailers can gain a competitive edge is by implementing supply chain analytics. This subchapter explores the numerous benefits that retailers can harness by incorporating supply chain analytics into their operations.

Improved Forecasting and Planning: Supply chain analytics provides retailers with valuable insights into customer demand patterns, allowing them to more accurately forecast and plan their inventory levels. By analyzing historical data and market trends, retailers can optimize their inventory management, reducing the risk of overstocking or stockouts. This leads to better customer satisfaction and increased sales.

Enhanced Operational Efficiency: Supply chain analytics helps retailers streamline their operations by identifying bottlenecks and inefficiencies in their supply chain processes. By analyzing data on lead times, transportation costs, and order fulfillment rates, retailers can make informed decisions to optimize their supply chain, resulting in reduced costs, improved productivity, and faster order fulfillment.

Optimized Pricing and Promotions: Supply chain analytics enables retailers to analyze pricing and promotional strategies to maximize profitability. By identifying the impact of various pricing scenarios and promotions on sales and margins, retailers can make data-driven decisions that optimize revenue while maintaining customer loyalty.

Improved Supplier Performance: With supply chain analytics, retailers can evaluate and monitor the performance of their suppliers. By analyzing data on delivery times, quality, and costs, retailers can identify the most reliable and cost-effective suppliers. This, in turn, helps to build stronger supplier relationships, reduce supply chain disruptions, and improve overall supply chain performance.

Enhanced Customer Experience: Supply chain analytics provides retailers with insights into customer preferences, behaviors, and buying patterns. By analyzing this data, retailers can personalize their offerings, improve product recommendations, and enhance the overall customer experience. This leads to increased customer satisfaction, loyalty, and repeat business.

Competitive Advantage: By leveraging supply chain analytics, retailers gain a significant competitive advantage over their rivals. The ability to make data-driven decisions, optimize operations, and deliver a superior customer experience sets retailers apart in a crowded market. Retailers that embrace supply chain analytics can adapt quickly to market changes, capitalize on emerging trends, and maintain a competitive edge.

In conclusion, implementing supply chain analytics in retail brings a multitude of benefits. This subchapter has highlighted improved forecasting and planning, enhanced operational efficiency, optimized pricing and promotions, improved supplier performance, enhanced customer experience, and a competitive advantage. By harnessing the power of supply chain analytics, retailers can optimize their operations, drive growth, and thrive in the dynamic retail landscape.

Challenges in Adopting Supply Chain Analytics in Retail

In today's competitive retail landscape, supply chain analytics has emerged as a powerful tool for retailers to optimize their operations, enhance customer satisfaction, and drive profitability. However, the adoption of supply chain analytics in the retail industry is not without its challenges. This subchapter explores the key obstacles that retailers face when implementing supply chain analytics and offers insights on how to overcome them.

One of the primary challenges in adopting supply chain analytics in retail is the availability and quality of data. Retailers often have vast amounts of data scattered across multiple systems, making it difficult to consolidate and analyze in a meaningful way. Additionally, the data may be incomplete, inconsistent, or outdated, resulting in inaccurate insights. To address this challenge, retailers need to invest in robust data management systems and ensure data accuracy and integrity through regular cleansing and validation processes.

Another challenge lies in the complexity of supply chain networks. Retail supply chains are often intricate, involving multiple suppliers, warehouses, distribution centers, and stores. Analyzing and optimizing such complex networks can be a daunting task. Retailers must develop advanced analytical models that can handle the complexity and provide actionable insights. Additionally, collaboration and information-sharing among supply chain partners are crucial to overcome this challenge, as it enables a holistic view and facilitates effective decision-making.

Furthermore, the lack of skilled resources, particularly business standard analysts, poses a challenge for retailers. Supply chain analytics requires a unique set of skills, including data analysis, statistical modeling, and domain knowledge. Retailers should invest in training and development programs to build a team of competent business standard analysts who can leverage supply chain analytics tools effectively.

In addition, there may be resistance to change within the organization. Implementing supply chain analytics often requires a shift in mindset and a cultural change. Some employees may be skeptical or resistant to the adoption of analytics-driven decision-making processes. Retailers need to communicate the benefits of supply chain analytics and involve employees in the implementation process to overcome this challenge successfully.

Lastly, cost considerations can also hinder the adoption of supply chain analytics in retail. Developing and implementing analytics solutions can be expensive, especially for small and medium-sized retailers. To address this challenge, retailers can consider partnering with technology providers or leveraging cloud-based analytics platforms that offer cost-effective solutions without compromising on functionality.

In conclusion, while the adoption of supply chain analytics in retail offers significant benefits, it is not without its challenges. By addressing the issues related to data, complexity, skills, change management, and cost, retailers can successfully overcome these obstacles and unlock the full potential of supply chain analytics to drive operational excellence and competitive advantage in the dynamic retail industry.

Chapter 2: Key Concepts in Supply Chain Analytics

Defining Supply Chain Analytics

In today's hyper-competitive retail landscape, the ability to make data-driven decisions is crucial for success. Supply chain analytics has emerged as a powerful tool that enables retailers to gain valuable insights, optimize operations, and drive profitability. This subchapter aims to provide a comprehensive understanding of supply chain analytics, its significance, and the benefits it offers to retailers.

Supply chain analytics can be defined as the process of collecting, analyzing, and interpreting data related to various aspects of the supply chain, including sourcing, procurement, inventory management, demand forecasting, logistics, and customer satisfaction. It involves leveraging advanced analytical techniques, such as data mining, predictive modeling, and machine learning, to uncover patterns, identify trends, and generate actionable insights.

For retailers, supply chain analytics serves as a strategic weapon to stay ahead of the competition. By harnessing the power of data, retailers can optimize their supply chain operations, reduce costs, improve customer satisfaction, and enhance overall efficiency. It enables them to make informed decisions regarding sourcing, inventory levels, transportation routes, and demand forecasting.

Business standard analysts play a pivotal role in implementing and utilizing supply chain analytics effectively. These professionals possess the expertise to extract meaningful insights from vast amounts of data, identify key performance indicators (KPIs), and develop sophisticated models to forecast demand accurately. By leveraging their skills, retailers can gain a competitive edge, improve decision-making processes, and drive revenue growth.

The benefits of supply chain analytics are manifold for retailers. Firstly, it enables them to identify inefficiencies and bottlenecks within their supply chain, allowing for targeted improvements and cost reductions. Secondly, by accurately forecasting demand, retailers can optimize inventory levels to meet customer needs while minimizing carrying costs. Thirdly, supply chain analytics helps retailers identify customer preferences and buying patterns, enabling them to tailor their offerings and enhance customer satisfaction.

In summary, supply chain analytics is a critical tool for retailers to gain insights, optimize operations, and drive profitability. By leveraging advanced analytical techniques, retailers can make informed decisions, reduce costs, improve efficiency, and enhance customer satisfaction. Business standard analysts play a crucial role in implementing and utilizing supply chain analytics effectively. By understanding the significance of supply chain analytics and harnessing its power, retailers can gain a competitive advantage in today's dynamic retail landscape.

Types of Data Used in Supply Chain Analytics

In today's data-driven business landscape, supply chain analytics has emerged as a crucial tool for retailers looking to optimize their operations and gain a competitive edge. By harnessing the power of data, retailers can make better decisions, streamline their supply chain processes, and ultimately improve their bottom line. However, to effectively leverage supply chain analytics, retailers must first understand the different types of data that are used in this field.

1. Transactional Data: Transactional data is at the core of supply chain analytics. It includes information about sales, purchases, shipments, and inventory levels. By analyzing transactional data, retailers can gain insights into demand patterns, identify bottlenecks, and optimize inventory management.

2. Customer Data: Understanding customer behavior is vital for retailers. Customer data includes information about preferences, purchasing habits, and demographics. By analyzing customer data, retailers can personalize their marketing strategies, forecast demand more accurately, and improve customer satisfaction.

3. External Data: External data refers to information obtained from outside sources. This can include weather data, economic indicators, social media sentiment analysis, or competitor pricing. By incorporating external data into their analytics models, retailers can gain a holistic view of their supply chain and make more informed decisions.

4. Sensor Data: With the rise of the Internet of Things (IoT), retailers can now collect real-time data from various sensors embedded in their

supply chain. This sensor data can provide valuable insights into factors such as temperature, humidity, location, and product condition. By monitoring sensor data, retailers can proactively address issues like spoilage, delays, or quality control problems.

5. Geospatial Data: Geospatial data involves location-based information such as maps, GPS coordinates, or transportation routes. By analyzing geospatial data, retailers can optimize their logistics and distribution networks, determine optimal store locations, and enhance route planning.

6. Financial Data: Financial data encompasses information about costs, budgets, and profitability. By analyzing financial data, retailers can identify areas of inefficiency, calculate the return on investment for various initiatives, and allocate resources more effectively.

By understanding and utilizing these different types of data, retailers can unlock the full potential of supply chain analytics. It is important for retailers to invest in robust data management systems and analytics tools that can handle large volumes of data and provide actionable insights. With the right data-driven approach, retailers can enhance their operational efficiency, improve customer satisfaction, and stay ahead in today's competitive retail landscape.

Key Performance Indicators in Retail Supply Chains

Key Performance Indicators (KPIs) in Retail Supply Chains

Introduction:
In today's highly competitive retail landscape, businesses are constantly striving to optimize their supply chain operations to gain a competitive edge. Key Performance Indicators (KPIs) play a crucial role in helping retailers measure their supply chain performance and identify areas for improvement. This subchapter aims to delve into the significance of KPIs in retail supply chains, providing valuable insights for retailers and business standard analysts seeking to optimize their operations.

Understanding Retail Supply Chain KPIs:
Retail supply chains encompass a complex network of activities, involving multiple stakeholders, from manufacturers and distributors to retailers and customers. To effectively manage and optimize this intricate web, retailers must rely on specific KPIs tailored to their unique needs. These KPIs provide quantifiable metrics that help evaluate the efficiency, cost-effectiveness, and customer satisfaction levels of supply chain operations.

Key Retail Supply Chain KPIs:
1. On-time Delivery: This KPI measures the percentage of deliveries made within the agreed-upon timeframe. It enables retailers to assess the reliability and punctuality of their suppliers and logistics partners, ensuring that products are available to meet customer demands.

2. Inventory Turnover: This KPI evaluates the speed at which inventory is sold and replenished. By analyzing inventory turnover,

retailers gain insights into their stock management efficiency, enabling them to avoid stockouts, minimize carrying costs, and optimize order quantities.

3. Order Accuracy: This KPI measures the accuracy of orders fulfilled, reflecting the percentage of orders delivered correctly and in full. High order accuracy ensures customer satisfaction, reduces returns, and minimizes operational costs associated with order rectification.

4. Perfect Order Rate: This KPI represents the percentage of orders that are fulfilled without any errors or issues, considering factors such as on-time delivery, order accuracy, and complete documentation. A higher perfect order rate indicates a more streamlined and reliable supply chain.

5. Cash-to-Cash Cycle Time: This KPI measures the time it takes for a retailer to convert its investments into cash flow. By analyzing this metric, retailers can identify bottlenecks in the supply chain that cause delays in receiving payments, allowing for better cash flow management.

Conclusion:

In the retail industry, optimizing supply chain operations is crucial to staying competitive and meeting customer expectations. Key Performance Indicators (KPIs) provide retailers with invaluable insights into their supply chain performance, enabling them to identify areas for improvement and make informed decisions. By tracking KPIs such as on-time delivery, inventory turnover, order accuracy, perfect order rate, and cash-to-cash cycle time, retailers and business standard analysts can enhance operational efficiency, reduce costs, and ultimately deliver an exceptional customer experience.

Predictive Analytics in Retail Supply Chains

In today's fast-paced retail industry, staying ahead of the competition requires more than just offering great products and services. It requires retailers to optimize their supply chains to ensure efficient operations, timely deliveries, and satisfied customers. This is where the power of predictive analytics comes into play.

Predictive analytics, a subset of data analytics, uses historical data, statistical algorithms, and machine learning techniques to forecast future events and trends. In the context of retail supply chains, predictive analytics can provide invaluable insights into demand patterns, inventory management, and overall supply chain performance. This subchapter explores the key benefits and applications of predictive analytics in the retail sector, helping retailers unlock their full potential.

One of the main advantages of predictive analytics in retail supply chains is the ability to accurately forecast customer demand. By analyzing historical data, demographic trends, and external factors such as weather patterns or economic indicators, retailers can anticipate fluctuations in demand for their products. This allows them to optimize inventory levels, reduce stockouts, and avoid excess inventory, ultimately improving customer satisfaction and minimizing costs.

Furthermore, predictive analytics can be used to optimize supply chain operations. By analyzing data from various sources, including point-of-sale systems, supplier records, and transportation data, retailers can identify bottlenecks, inefficiencies, and potential disruptions in their supply chains. Armed with this knowledge, they can make informed decisions regarding production, distribution, and logistics, ensuring smooth operations and timely deliveries.

For business standard analysts, understanding and leveraging predictive analytics is crucial in today's retail landscape. By harnessing the power of data and statistical models, these analysts can provide retailers with accurate forecasts, actionable insights, and optimization strategies. This not only enhances their value as analysts but also helps retailers make data-driven decisions that drive business growth and profitability.

In conclusion, predictive analytics is a game-changer for retailers looking to optimize their supply chains and gain a competitive edge. By accurately forecasting customer demand and optimizing operations, retailers can enhance customer satisfaction, reduce costs, and improve overall business performance. Business standard analysts play a vital role in harnessing the power of predictive analytics, helping retailers unlock the full potential of their supply chains. Embracing this technology is no longer an option but a necessity for retailers aiming to thrive in today's dynamic retail landscape.

Chapter 3: Data Collection and Management for Supply Chain Analytics

Collecting Relevant Data for Supply Chain Analytics

In today's highly competitive retail landscape, supply chain analytics has emerged as a powerful tool for retailers to gain a competitive edge. By leveraging data and advanced analytics techniques, retailers can unlock valuable insights that drive operational efficiency, improve customer satisfaction, and increase profitability. However, to harness the full potential of supply chain analytics, retailers must first focus on collecting relevant data.

Data forms the foundation of any successful supply chain analytics initiative. Without accurate and comprehensive data, retailers will struggle to gain meaningful insights and make informed decisions. Therefore, it is crucial for retailers to establish robust data collection processes that capture the necessary information at every stage of the supply chain.

The first step in collecting relevant data is to identify the key performance indicators (KPIs) that align with the retailer's goals and objectives. These KPIs may vary depending on the nature of the business, but common metrics include on-time delivery, order fulfillment rate, inventory turnover, and customer satisfaction. By defining these KPIs, retailers can determine the types of data that need to be collected.

Once the KPIs are established, retailers should identify the sources of data within their supply chain. This can include internal systems such as enterprise resource planning (ERP) software, warehouse management systems, and point-of-sale (POS) systems. Additionally, external sources such as supplier data, market trends, and customer feedback should also be considered. By integrating data from various sources, retailers can gain a comprehensive view of their supply chain performance.

It is important to ensure the accuracy and reliability of the collected data. This can be achieved through data cleansing, which involves removing duplicate records, correcting errors, and standardizing formats. Retailers should also establish data governance policies that define data ownership, access rights, and data quality standards. Regular audits and checks should be conducted to maintain data integrity.

Furthermore, retailers should consider leveraging emerging technologies such as the Internet of Things (IoT) devices and sensors to collect real-time data. These technologies can provide valuable insights into inventory levels, transportation conditions, and customer behavior, enabling retailers to optimize their supply chain operations and enhance the overall customer experience.

In conclusion, collecting relevant data is a crucial step in harnessing the power of supply chain analytics for retailers. By identifying key performance indicators, integrating data from various sources, ensuring data accuracy, and leveraging emerging technologies, retailers can unlock valuable insights and drive operational excellence. With a well-established data collection process, retailers can make informed decisions that improve efficiency, reduce costs, and ultimately deliver a superior customer experience.

Data Quality and Validation Techniques

In today's fast-paced and data-driven retail industry, accurate and reliable data is crucial for making informed business decisions. Data quality and validation techniques play a vital role in ensuring that retailers have access to high-quality data that can be trusted to drive effective supply chain analytics and optimization strategies.

Data quality refers to the accuracy, completeness, consistency, and timeliness of the data. Poor data quality can lead to flawed analysis, erroneous insights, and ultimately, ineffective decision-making. To overcome such challenges, retailers need to implement robust data validation techniques.

One of the most common data validation techniques used by business standard analysts is data profiling. This technique involves analyzing the data to understand its structure, content, and quality. By examining data patterns, values, and distributions, analysts can identify anomalies, inconsistencies, and errors. Data profiling helps retailers gain a comprehensive understanding of their data, enabling them to identify and rectify any issues that may impact its quality.

Another important technique for data quality and validation is data cleansing. This process involves identifying and correcting or removing errors, inconsistencies, and inaccuracies from the data. Data cleansing techniques can range from basic data formatting and standardization to more complex methods such as outlier detection and data imputation. By cleaning the data, retailers can ensure that the information used for analysis and optimization is accurate and reliable.

Data validation also includes techniques such as data reconciliation and data auditing. Data reconciliation involves comparing data from different sources or systems to identify discrepancies and ensure consistency. It helps retailers identify and resolve data integration issues, ensuring that the data used for analysis is complete and accurate. Data auditing involves conducting regular checks to verify the accuracy and reliability of the data. By establishing data auditing processes, retailers can proactively identify and address data quality issues.

In conclusion, data quality and validation techniques are essential for retailers and business standard analysts in the retail industry. Accurate and reliable data is the foundation for effective supply chain analytics and optimization. By implementing robust data profiling, data cleansing, data reconciliation, and data auditing techniques, retailers can ensure that their data is of high quality, enabling them to make informed decisions that drive business growth and success.

Data Storage and Retrieval Methods

In today's digital age, data has become an invaluable asset for retailers. The ability to store and retrieve vast amounts of data efficiently is crucial for making informed business decisions and optimizing supply chain operations. This subchapter aims to provide retailers, specifically business standard analysts, with an overview of various data storage and retrieval methods that can enhance their understanding and utilization of supply chain analytics.

One of the most common methods of data storage is the use of relational databases. These databases store data in tables with predefined relationships between them, allowing for efficient data retrieval through structured query language (SQL). Retailers can leverage relational databases to store customer data, sales records, and inventory information, enabling them to analyze trends and make data-driven decisions.

Another method gaining popularity is the use of cloud storage. With the advent of cloud computing, retailers can now store and access their data remotely, eliminating the need for physical servers. Cloud storage offers scalability, flexibility, and cost-effectiveness, making it an ideal solution for retailers of all sizes. Additionally, cloud storage providers often offer advanced analytics tools and machine learning capabilities, enabling retailers to extract valuable insights from their data.

For retailers dealing with large volumes of unstructured data, such as social media posts or customer reviews, NoSQL databases are a valuable option. NoSQL databases are designed to handle unstructured and semi-structured data efficiently, allowing retailers to store and retrieve data in a flexible manner. This method is particularly useful for sentiment analysis, customer sentiment tracking, and monitoring brand reputation.

In recent years, the adoption of data lakes has also gained traction in the retail industry. A data lake is a centralized repository that can store both structured and unstructured data in its raw form. It offers retailers the ability to store massive amounts of data without the need for upfront data modeling. Data lakes can be integrated with advanced analytics tools, enabling retailers to explore and analyze their data in real-time, uncovering valuable insights and trends.

In conclusion, choosing the right data storage and retrieval methods is crucial for retailers looking to optimize their supply chain analytics. Whether it be relational databases, cloud storage, NoSQL databases, or data lakes, each method offers unique advantages and can be tailored to the specific needs of retailers. By effectively storing and retrieving data, retailers can gain a competitive edge in the market, enhance their decision-making processes, and ultimately drive business growth.

Data Security and Privacy Concerns in Retail Supply Chains

In today's data-driven world, retailers are increasingly relying on supply chain analytics and optimization to gain a competitive edge. While these technologies offer tremendous benefits, they also bring along significant data security and privacy concerns that retailers must address to protect their businesses and customers.

One of the major concerns in retail supply chains is the risk of data breaches. With the increasing volume of sensitive information being exchanged between retailers, suppliers, logistics partners, and customers, the likelihood of unauthorized access and data theft is higher than ever before. A breach can result in severe financial losses, damage to reputation, and legal repercussions. Therefore, retailers must establish robust security measures, such as encryption, authentication protocols, and firewalls, to safeguard their data from external threats.

Another critical concern revolves around ensuring privacy in the collection and use of customer data. Retailers often collect large amounts of customer information, including purchase history, preferences, and personal details, to personalize the shopping experience and improve supply chain efficiency. However, this data can be vulnerable to misuse or unauthorized access, leading to privacy violations. Retailers must obtain explicit consent from customers for data collection, clearly communicate their data usage policies, and implement strict data access controls within their organizations to protect customer privacy.

Additionally, the increasing use of advanced technologies like Internet of Things (IoT) devices and artificial intelligence (AI) in retail supply chains raises unique security challenges. IoT devices, such as smart shelves and RFID tags, generate vast amounts of real-time data that can be valuable to cybercriminals if not properly secured. AI algorithms, while providing valuable insights, can also be vulnerable to manipulation and bias. Retailers must implement comprehensive security measures, including regular software updates, network segmentation, and continuous monitoring, to mitigate these risks and ensure the integrity of their supply chain analytics.

To address these data security and privacy concerns effectively, retailers need to invest in robust cybersecurity infrastructure, establish clear data governance policies, and educate their employees about best practices for data protection. Collaboration with industry experts, such as business standard analysts, can help retailers stay updated on the latest security threats and mitigation strategies.

In conclusion, as retailers embrace supply chain analytics and optimization, they must also prioritize data security and privacy. By implementing robust security measures, ensuring customer privacy, and addressing the unique challenges posed by advanced technologies, retailers can protect their businesses, build trust with customers, and maximize the benefits of data-driven supply chain management.

Chapter 4: Analytical Techniques for Supply Chain Optimization

Descriptive Analytics in Retail Supply Chains

In today's competitive retail landscape, businesses are constantly striving to gain a deeper understanding of their supply chains to drive efficiency, reduce costs, and ultimately improve customer satisfaction. Descriptive analytics plays a crucial role in helping retailers achieve these goals. This subchapter of "The Retailer's Guide to Supply Chain Analytics and Optimization" will provide retailers, particularly business standard analysts, with an in-depth understanding of descriptive analytics in retail supply chains and how it can be leveraged to enhance their operations.

Descriptive analytics involves analyzing historical data to gain insights into past performance and trends. In the context of retail supply chains, it enables retailers to examine their operations, identify patterns, and uncover valuable information about various aspects of the supply chain, including procurement, inventory management, transportation, and demand forecasting.

One of the key benefits of descriptive analytics is its ability to provide retailers with a comprehensive overview of their supply chain performance. By analyzing data on key performance indicators (KPIs) such as on-time delivery, stockouts, and inventory turnover, retailers can assess their current state and identify areas for improvement. For instance, descriptive analytics can reveal whether certain suppliers consistently deliver late or if certain products face higher demand during specific seasons.

Moreover, descriptive analytics helps retailers detect inefficiencies and bottlenecks within their supply chains. Through data visualization techniques, such as dashboards and reports, business standard analysts can easily identify areas where processes are prone to delays, excess inventory, or waste. Armed with this information, retailers can take proactive measures to optimize their supply chain operations, streamline processes, and reduce costs.

Descriptive analytics also empowers retailers to make data-driven decisions. By analyzing data on customer preferences, buying patterns, and market trends, retailers can gain insights into consumer behavior and adjust their inventory levels accordingly. This enables them to meet customer demand more effectively, minimize stockouts, and reduce excess inventory.

In conclusion, descriptive analytics is a powerful tool for retailers and business standard analysts seeking to optimize their supply chain operations. By leveraging historical data, retailers can gain valuable insights into their supply chain performance, detect inefficiencies, and make informed decisions. With the ability to identify trends and patterns, retailers can improve their overall operational efficiency, reduce costs, and enhance customer satisfaction. By embracing descriptive analytics, retailers can stay ahead in the ever-evolving retail industry.

Diagnostic Analytics for Identifying Supply Chain Issues

In today's fast-paced retail landscape, supply chain issues can arise at any time and have a significant impact on a retailer's bottom line. Identifying and resolving these issues swiftly is crucial to maintaining customer satisfaction and maximizing profitability. This subchapter aims to provide retailers, particularly business standard analysts, with insights into the power of diagnostic analytics in identifying and resolving supply chain issues effectively.

Diagnostic analytics refers to the use of advanced data analysis techniques to examine historical data and uncover the root causes of problems. By leveraging this powerful tool, retailers can gain actionable insights into their supply chain operations, enabling them to make informed decisions and drive continuous improvement.

One of the primary benefits of diagnostic analytics is its ability to pinpoint inefficiencies and bottlenecks within the supply chain. By analyzing data on key performance indicators (KPIs) such as order fulfillment rates, inventory turnover, and delivery times, retailers can identify areas that require attention. For instance, if there is a consistent delay in delivering products to customers, diagnostic analytics can help trace the root cause, whether it be a problem with the warehouse layout, transportation network, or order processing system.

Moreover, diagnostic analytics can also uncover hidden patterns and correlations that may be contributing to supply chain issues. By examining data from various sources such as sales, customer feedback, and market trends, retailers can identify factors that affect demand and supply. This insight can help them adjust inventory levels, optimize production schedules, and ensure the availability of popular products during peak seasons.

Another valuable application of diagnostic analytics is in risk management. By analyzing historical data and external factors such as weather patterns, economic trends, and supplier performance, retailers can proactively identify potential risks and devise contingency plans. For example, if a retailer relies heavily on a single supplier for a critical product, diagnostic analytics can help identify alternative suppliers to mitigate the risk of disruptions.

In conclusion, diagnostic analytics is a valuable tool for retailers, especially business standard analysts, to identify and address supply chain issues effectively. By leveraging advanced data analysis techniques, retailers can uncover inefficiencies, identify hidden patterns, and manage risks. Ultimately, the application of diagnostic analytics in supply chain operations can lead to improved customer satisfaction, increased profitability, and a competitive edge in the dynamic retail industry.

Predictive Analytics for Demand Forecasting

In today's highly competitive retail industry, accurately forecasting demand is crucial for optimizing inventory levels and ensuring customer satisfaction. Traditional forecasting methods often fall short in capturing the complex and dynamic nature of consumer behavior. That's where predictive analytics comes into play – a powerful tool that leverages historical data and advanced statistical models to forecast future demand with greater accuracy and precision.

This subchapter explores the concept of predictive analytics for demand forecasting and its practical application in the retail industry. Addressed to retailers and business standard analysts, it aims to demystify this cutting-edge technique and highlight its potential for driving operational efficiency and profitability.

The chapter begins by introducing the fundamentals of predictive analytics, explaining how it incorporates various data sources, such as sales history, customer demographics, economic indicators, and external factors like weather patterns or social media trends. It emphasizes the importance of data quality, highlighting the need for retailers to invest in robust data management systems and analytics tools.

Next, the subchapter delves into the key techniques and models used in predictive analytics for demand forecasting. It discusses time series analysis, regression analysis, and machine learning algorithms, providing real-world examples of how these methods have been successfully employed by retailers to predict demand patterns. It also sheds light on the challenges and limitations of each technique, helping retailers make informed decisions about the most suitable approach for their specific needs.

Furthermore, the subchapter explores the benefits of leveraging predictive analytics for demand forecasting in the retail context. It emphasizes how accurate demand forecasts can optimize inventory levels, reduce stockouts or overstocks, and streamline supply chain operations. It also highlights how predictive analytics can enhance customer experience by ensuring product availability, enabling personalized marketing campaigns, and facilitating demand-driven pricing strategies.

To conclude, this subchapter emphasizes the transformative potential of predictive analytics for demand forecasting in the retail industry. It urges retailers and business standard analysts to embrace this technology-driven approach to gain a competitive edge in today's volatile market. By harnessing the power of predictive analytics, retailers can unlock insights, make data-driven decisions, and create a demand-centric supply chain that meets the ever-evolving needs of their customers.

Prescriptive Analytics for Optimal Decision Making

In today's rapidly evolving retail landscape, making data-driven decisions has become more crucial than ever. As a retailer, you need to not only analyze vast amounts of data but also leverage it to gain actionable insights and make optimal decisions that can propel your business forward. This is where prescriptive analytics comes into play.

Prescriptive analytics is a powerful tool that goes beyond descriptive and predictive analytics. While descriptive analytics helps you understand what happened and predictive analytics informs you about what might happen, prescriptive analytics takes it a step further by recommending the best course of action to achieve your desired outcomes.

For retailers, prescriptive analytics can be a game-changer. It enables you to optimize various aspects of your supply chain, including inventory management, demand forecasting, pricing strategies, and more. By leveraging this advanced analytical technique, you can make data-backed decisions that ultimately drive profitability and enhance customer satisfaction.

One of the key advantages of prescriptive analytics is its ability to consider multiple variables and constraints simultaneously. For instance, when determining optimal inventory levels, prescriptive analytics takes into account factors such as sales trends, seasonality, supplier lead times, and customer demand patterns. It then recommends the best order quantities and replenishment schedules to ensure optimal inventory levels while minimizing costs and reducing stockouts.

Moreover, prescriptive analytics can help retailers optimize their pricing strategies. By analyzing historical sales data, competitor pricing, and customer behavior, prescriptive analytics can recommend the most profitable pricing structures. It can also provide insights on how to dynamically adjust prices based on factors like demand fluctuations, competitor actions, and market conditions.

Prescriptive analytics can also assist retailers in supply chain optimization. By considering various factors such as transportation costs, order fulfillment time, and customer location, prescriptive analytics can recommend the most efficient routes, warehouse locations, and distribution strategies. This not only minimizes costs but also improves delivery speed and customer satisfaction.

As a business standard analyst in the retail industry, mastering prescriptive analytics can significantly enhance your decision-making capabilities. By effectively utilizing this advanced analytical technique, you can identify hidden opportunities, uncover potential risks, and make informed choices that drive growth and competitive advantage for your organization.

In conclusion, prescriptive analytics is a powerful tool for retailers, enabling them to make optimal decisions and drive business success. By leveraging this advanced analytical technique, retailers can gain a competitive edge in today's dynamic marketplace. Whether it's inventory management, pricing strategies, or supply chain optimization, prescriptive analytics can provide valuable insights and recommendations for optimal decision-making. Embracing prescriptive analytics is essential for retailers looking to stay ahead of the curve and achieve sustainable growth in the ever-evolving retail industry.

Chapter 5: Implementing Supply Chain Analytics in Retail

Steps to Successful Implementation of Supply Chain Analytics

In today's rapidly evolving retail landscape, the ability to extract meaningful insights from data has become crucial for staying competitive. Supply chain analytics, when implemented effectively, can provide retailers with a competitive edge by optimizing operations, reducing costs, and enhancing customer satisfaction. However, successfully implementing supply chain analytics requires careful planning and execution. In this subchapter, we will outline the key steps to ensure a successful implementation of supply chain analytics, specifically tailored for retailers and business standard analysts.

1. Define Clear Objectives: Before diving into the implementation process, it is essential to define clear objectives for your supply chain analytics initiative. Determine what specific areas of your supply chain you want to improve, such as inventory management, demand forecasting, or transportation optimization. Clearly outlining your goals will help you stay focused throughout the implementation process.

2. Establish Data Infrastructure: To leverage the power of analytics, you need to ensure you have a robust data infrastructure in place. This includes collecting and consolidating data from various sources within your supply chain, such as sales data, inventory data, and customer data. Implementing data management systems and tools that can handle large volumes of data and provide real-time insights is crucial.

3. Identify Key Performance Indicators (KPIs): Identify the key performance indicators that will help you measure the success of your supply chain analytics initiative. These KPIs can vary depending on your specific objectives but may include metrics such as order fulfillment rate, inventory turnover, or on-time delivery. Establishing KPIs will allow you to track progress and make data-driven decisions.

4. Select Suitable Analytics Tools: There is a wide range of analytics tools available in the market, each with its own strengths and capabilities. Evaluate different tools based on your requirements, such as ease of use, scalability, and integration capabilities with your existing systems. Consider partnering with analytics providers who specialize in the retail industry to ensure a tailored solution.

5. Build Analytical Capabilities: Implementing supply chain analytics requires skilled analysts who can interpret and derive insights from data. Invest in training programs or hiring experienced data analysts who understand the intricacies of the retail industry. Building a team with strong analytical capabilities will enable you to extract actionable insights from your data.

6. Test and Refine: Before fully deploying your supply chain analytics solution, conduct pilot tests to ensure its effectiveness. Start with a small subset of data and evaluate the results. Use this testing phase to identify any potential issues or areas for improvement and refine your approach accordingly.

7. Continuously Monitor and Improve: Supply chain analytics is an ongoing process. Continuously monitor the performance of your supply chain and make adjustments as needed to optimize operations

further. Regularly review KPIs, analyze trends, and leverage insights to identify potential areas for improvement.

By following these steps, retailers and business standard analysts can successfully implement supply chain analytics, transforming their operations into data-driven, efficient, and customer-centric supply chains. Embrace the power of analytics and gain a competitive edge in the dynamic retail industry.

Building an Analytics Team in Retail Organizations

In today's highly competitive retail industry, data analytics has become increasingly crucial for success. With the ever-increasing amounts of data being generated, retailers must harness the power of analytics to gain valuable insights and make informed decisions. This subchapter aims to guide retailers in building an effective analytics team specifically tailored to their needs.

A successful analytics team in a retail organization requires a diverse skill set, with the business standard analyst playing a pivotal role. These professionals possess a deep understanding of both business operations and data analytics techniques. They are adept at translating complex data into actionable insights that drive strategic decision-making.

The first step in building an analytics team is to identify the specific goals and objectives of the retail organization. This will help determine the required skills and expertise of the team members. For instance, if the retailer aims to optimize supply chain operations, analysts with expertise in inventory management and logistics should be considered.

Once the desired skill set is identified, retailers should focus on recruiting and hiring individuals with a strong analytical background. This may involve partnering with universities, attending job fairs, or leveraging professional networking platforms. Additionally, it is essential to screen candidates for their technical proficiency, problem-solving abilities, and business acumen.

To foster a collaborative environment, retailers should encourage cross-functional collaboration between the analytics team and other departments within the organization. This can be achieved through regular meetings, knowledge-sharing sessions, and joint projects. By integrating analytics into various business functions, retailers can unlock new opportunities for growth and optimization.

In addition to technical skills, it is important for the analytics team to possess strong communication and presentation abilities. They should be able to convey complex findings in a clear and concise manner to non-technical stakeholders. This ensures that the insights generated by the analytics team are effectively utilized by decision-makers across the organization.

Continuous learning and development should be a priority for the analytics team. Retailers should provide access to training programs, industry conferences, and online resources to enhance their skills and stay updated with the latest advancements in analytics tools and techniques.

In conclusion, building an analytics team is crucial for retailers looking to leverage data-driven insights to optimize their supply chain operations. By recruiting skilled business standard analysts and fostering a collaborative environment, retailers can unlock the full potential of analytics and gain a competitive edge in the retail industry.

Selecting and Implementing Analytical Tools and Technologies

In today's competitive retail landscape, data-driven decision-making is the key to staying ahead of the curve. As a retailer, it is crucial to invest in the right analytical tools and technologies that can help you optimize your supply chain operations and boost your bottom line. This subchapter will guide you through the process of selecting and implementing these tools, providing valuable insights for business standard analysts like yourself.

The first step in this journey is understanding your specific needs and objectives. Identifying the areas of your supply chain that require improvement will help you narrow down the selection of analytical tools. Whether it's inventory management, demand forecasting, or transportation optimization, having a clear understanding of your goals will enable you to choose the most suitable tools for your business.

Once you have defined your requirements, it's time to research the available options. There is a wide range of analytical tools and technologies in the market, each offering unique features and capabilities. Consider factors such as scalability, ease of use, integration capabilities, and cost-effectiveness when evaluating different solutions. Don't forget to also consult industry experts and attend conferences to stay updated on the latest trends and innovations.

After shortlisting potential tools, it's important to thoroughly assess their compatibility with your existing systems and infrastructure. Integration is a critical aspect that should not be overlooked. The selected tools should seamlessly integrate with your current technology stack to ensure smooth implementation and data flow. Additionally, consider the learning curve associated with each tool and the availability of training resources to enable your team to maximize its potential.

Once you have made your selection, it's time to implement the chosen analytical tools. This process should be carefully planned and executed to minimize disruptions to your supply chain operations. Collaboration between your IT department, data analysts, and other stakeholders is crucial for a successful implementation. Adequate training should be provided to ensure that your team members can effectively utilize the tools and generate actionable insights from the data.

In conclusion, selecting and implementing analytical tools and technologies is a critical step in harnessing the power of supply chain analytics for retailers. By understanding your specific needs, conducting thorough research, evaluating compatibility, and executing a well-planned implementation strategy, you can empower your business standard analysts to make data-driven decisions that drive efficiency and profitability in your retail operations.

Integrating Supply Chain Analytics with Existing Systems

In today's competitive retail landscape, staying ahead of the game requires retailers to make data-driven decisions and optimize their supply chain operations. To achieve this, the integration of supply chain analytics with existing systems becomes a crucial step for retailers. By harnessing the power of data and technology, retailers can gain valuable insights and streamline their operations, ultimately leading to improved efficiency, reduced costs, and increased customer satisfaction.

Supply chain analytics refers to the use of advanced analytics techniques, such as predictive modeling, machine learning, and data visualization, to analyze and interpret vast amounts of supply chain data. By leveraging these analytics capabilities, retailers can uncover hidden patterns, identify bottlenecks, and make informed decisions that drive operational excellence.

However, to fully realize the potential of supply chain analytics, it is essential to integrate these analytics capabilities with existing systems. This integration allows retailers to leverage their existing data sources, such as enterprise resource planning (ERP) systems, customer relationship management (CRM) systems, and point-of-sale (POS) systems, to generate comprehensive insights.

Integrating supply chain analytics with existing systems brings several benefits to retailers. Firstly, it enables real-time data synchronization, ensuring that the analytics models and reports are up-to-date and accurate. This real-time visibility into the supply chain allows retailers to respond quickly to changing market trends and customer demands, reducing stock-outs and overstock situations.

Secondly, integration enables seamless data flow between different systems, eliminating manual data entry and reducing the risk of errors. This automation saves time and resources, enabling the retail staff to focus on value-added activities rather than mundane administrative tasks.

Furthermore, integration allows retailers to create a holistic view of their supply chain operations by combining data from various sources. This comprehensive view enables them to identify opportunities for optimization, such as optimizing inventory levels, improving transportation routes, or enhancing supplier performance.

To successfully integrate supply chain analytics with existing systems, retailers need to invest in the right technology infrastructure and ensure data compatibility and consistency across different systems. They should also consider the scalability and flexibility of the analytics platform, as their business requirements may evolve over time.

In conclusion, integrating supply chain analytics with existing systems is a critical step for retailers aiming to optimize their operations and gain a competitive edge. By leveraging the power of data and technology, retailers can uncover valuable insights, streamline their supply chain processes, and ultimately deliver better customer experiences.

Chapter 6: Case Studies in Retail Supply Chain Analytics

Case Study 1: Optimizing Inventory Management with Analytics

In today's competitive retail landscape, effective inventory management is crucial for retailers to stay ahead of the game. With the advent of advanced analytics, retailers now have the tools to optimize their inventory management processes, improve customer satisfaction, and boost profitability. This case study delves into a real-life example of how analytics can transform inventory management for the better.

The Scenario:
A well-established retail chain was grappling with the challenges of excess inventory and stockouts. Their manual inventory management system was not only time-consuming but also prone to errors, leading to inefficient operations and dissatisfied customers. The company recognized the need for a data-driven approach to inventory management and turned to analytics for a solution.

The Analytics Solution:
The retailer engaged a team of business standard analysts to develop an analytics-driven inventory management system. Leveraging historical sales data, customer preferences, and market trends, the team used advanced forecasting models to predict demand accurately. These forecasts enabled the retailer to optimize their inventory levels, ensuring the right products were available at the right time and in the right quantities.

Furthermore, the analytics solution incorporated real-time data from point-of-sale systems, allowing the retailer to monitor inventory levels and demand patterns continuously. By analyzing this data, the retailer could identify slow-moving items, adjust their pricing strategies, and avoid overstocking or stockouts.

The Results:
By implementing the analytics-driven inventory management system, the retailer experienced remarkable improvements across various key performance indicators. Firstly, excess inventory was significantly reduced, resulting in cost savings and increased cash flow. The retailer could identify slow-moving items promptly and take proactive measures to liquidate them, minimizing losses.

Secondly, stockouts were greatly reduced, leading to improved customer satisfaction and loyalty. Customers could find their desired products consistently, eliminating frustration and the need to shop elsewhere. Consequently, the retailer saw increased sales and customer retention, contributing to overall business growth.

Moreover, the analytics solution enabled the retailer to optimize their replenishment cycles and reduce lead times. By accurately predicting demand, they could place orders with suppliers in a timely manner, ensuring a seamless flow of inventory and minimizing disruptions in the supply chain.

In conclusion, the successful implementation of analytics in inventory management transformed the retailer's operations, resulting in cost savings, increased sales, and improved customer satisfaction. This case study highlights the power of analytics in optimizing inventory management for retailers. By leveraging data and advanced forecasting models, retailers can make informed decisions, stay agile, and gain a competitive edge in the dynamic retail industry.

Case Study 2: Improving Supply Chain Efficiency through Predictive Analytics

In today's competitive retail landscape, optimizing supply chain operations is crucial to gain a competitive edge. Retailers need to constantly evaluate and enhance their supply chain processes to meet customer demands efficiently. This case study explores how predictive analytics can drive significant improvements in supply chain efficiency, enabling retailers to make better-informed decisions and achieve higher profitability.

Introduction:

As retailers face growing challenges in managing complex supply chains, the role of predictive analytics becomes even more critical. By leveraging advanced data analysis techniques, retailers can gain valuable insights into their supply chain operations, identify bottlenecks, and predict future demand patterns. This case study presents a real-world example of how a retailer successfully improved its supply chain efficiency using predictive analytics.

Problem Statement:

Our featured retailer, faced with rising operational costs and inconsistent inventory levels, sought to optimize its supply chain to minimize stockouts, reduce inventory carrying costs, and improve overall operational efficiency. The retailer realized the need to leverage predictive analytics to gain a competitive advantage in the market.

Solution:

The retailer implemented a predictive analytics solution that integrated historical sales data, customer behavior data, and external factors such as seasonality and promotions. By leveraging machine learning algorithms and data modeling techniques, the retailer was able to identify demand patterns, forecast customer preferences, and optimize inventory levels accordingly.

Results:

By adopting predictive analytics, the retailer achieved significant improvements in its supply chain efficiency. The retailer was able to reduce stockouts by accurately predicting demand and optimizing replenishment cycles. This not only improved customer satisfaction but also reduced inventory carrying costs. Additionally, the retailer gained insights into customer preferences, enabling targeted marketing campaigns and personalized promotions.

Conclusion:

This case study demonstrates the transformative power of predictive analytics in enhancing supply chain efficiency for retailers. By leveraging advanced data analysis techniques, retailers can gain valuable insights into demand patterns, optimize inventory levels, and make data-driven decisions. As a business standard analyst, it is essential to understand the potential of predictive analytics in improving supply chain operations and its role in driving profitability for retail businesses. By embracing predictive analytics, retailers can stay ahead of the competition, enhance customer satisfaction, and achieve sustainable growth in the dynamic retail industry.

Case Study 3: Enhancing Customer Satisfaction with Prescriptive Analytics

In today's competitive retail landscape, understanding and meeting customer expectations is crucial for success. This case study explores how prescriptive analytics can enhance customer satisfaction and drive business growth for retailers. By leveraging the power of data-driven insights, retailers can make informed decisions, optimize their supply chain, and deliver a seamless shopping experience to their customers.

Prescriptive analytics is an advanced analytics technique that goes beyond descriptive and predictive analytics. It not only provides insights into what has happened and what is likely to happen but also recommends the best course of action to achieve desired outcomes. For retailers, this means being able to proactively address customer needs and preferences.

In this case study, we will focus on a business standard analyst working for a retail company that experienced a decline in customer satisfaction scores. By utilizing prescriptive analytics, the analyst was able to identify the root causes of dissatisfaction, develop targeted strategies, and ultimately improve customer satisfaction.

The first step was to gather and analyze data from various sources, such as customer feedback, sales data, and supply chain information. With the help of advanced analytics tools, the analyst uncovered key insights, including product availability issues, long delivery times, and inconsistent pricing.

Using these insights, the analyst developed a prescriptive analytics model that recommended specific actions to enhance customer satisfaction. For instance, the model suggested optimizing inventory levels to ensure product availability, streamlining the delivery process to reduce wait times, and implementing dynamic pricing strategies to maintain competitiveness.

By implementing these recommendations, the retail company witnessed significant improvements in customer satisfaction scores. Customers appreciated the increased product availability, shorter delivery times, and more competitive pricing. As a result, customer loyalty and repeat purchases increased, leading to higher sales revenue and market share.

This case study demonstrates the power of prescriptive analytics in driving customer satisfaction and business growth. By leveraging data and advanced analytics techniques, retailers can gain valuable insights into customer preferences and behavior. Armed with these insights, they can make data-driven decisions to optimize their supply chain, improve customer service, and ultimately enhance the overall shopping experience.

In conclusion, prescriptive analytics is a valuable tool for retailers seeking to enhance customer satisfaction. By understanding and meeting customer expectations, retailers can gain a competitive edge in today's dynamic market. By investing in advanced analytics capabilities and leveraging the power of data-driven insights, retailers can optimize their supply chain, drive customer loyalty, and achieve long-term success.

Case Study 4: Overcoming Challenges in Implementing Supply Chain Analytics

Introduction:

In the rapidly evolving world of retail, staying competitive requires retailers to adapt to changing consumer demands and market trends. To achieve this, retailers are increasingly turning to supply chain analytics to gain valuable insights and optimize their operations. However, implementing supply chain analytics can present several challenges that need to be overcome to ensure successful integration and utilization. This case study explores the hurdles faced by retailers and provides practical solutions to overcome them.

Identifying Key Challenges:

1. Data Integration: Retailers often struggle with the integration of vast amounts of data from various sources. Siloed systems and inconsistent data formats hinder the ability to derive meaningful insights. Additionally, the lack of data governance practices can lead to inaccuracies and incomplete data sets.

2. Analytical Skills Gap: Retailers may lack the necessary analytical skills within their workforce to effectively interpret and utilize supply chain analytics. Business standard analysts are crucial in bridging this gap and ensuring that data-driven insights are effectively communicated to decision-makers.

3. Resistance to Change: Implementing supply chain analytics requires a shift in mindset and a willingness to embrace new technologies and processes. Resistance to change from employees and stakeholders can

hinder progress and limit the potential benefits of analytics implementation.

Overcoming Challenges:

1. Data Integration: Retailers must invest in robust data management systems that enable seamless integration of data from various sources. Implementing data governance practices ensures data accuracy and consistency. Collaborating with technology partners can provide innovative solutions to data integration challenges.

2. Analytical Skills Gap: Retailers should invest in training programs to upskill their business standard analysts, empowering them with the necessary tools and techniques to effectively analyze and interpret supply chain data. Collaborating with educational institutions or hiring external experts can also address this skills gap.

3. Resistance to Change: Retailers need to communicate the value and benefits of supply chain analytics to employees and stakeholders. Demonstrating success stories and highlighting the positive impact on operational efficiency and customer satisfaction can help alleviate resistance. Involving employees in the process and empowering them to contribute to decision-making can foster a sense of ownership and support for the changes.

Conclusion:

Implementing supply chain analytics in the retail industry offers immense opportunities for optimization and competitive advantage. However, retailers must be prepared to address the challenges that come with this transformation. By investing in robust data management systems, upskilling business standard analysts, and fostering a culture of change and innovation, retailers can overcome these challenges and unlock the full potential of supply chain analytics. Embracing these solutions will enable retailers to make data-driven decisions, optimize operations, and ultimately enhance customer experiences in the dynamic and ever-evolving retail landscape.

Chapter 7: Future Trends in Supply Chain Analytics for Retailers

Emerging Technologies in Supply Chain Analytics

In today's fast-paced and highly competitive retail industry, incorporating advanced technologies into supply chain analytics has become imperative for success. Retailers need to stay ahead of the curve and leverage innovative solutions to optimize their supply chain operations. This subchapter explores the latest emerging technologies that are transforming supply chain analytics, providing valuable insights for retailers and business standard analysts.

One of the most significant emerging technologies in supply chain analytics is artificial intelligence (AI). AI-powered algorithms can analyze vast amounts of data to identify patterns, trends, and anomalies, enabling retailers to make informed decisions in real-time. Machine learning algorithms, a subset of AI, can continuously learn from data and improve forecasting accuracy, demand planning, and inventory optimization.

Another game-changing technology is blockchain. Traditionally associated with cryptocurrencies, blockchain can revolutionize supply chain management by providing transparency, traceability, and security. Retailers can track products through every stage of the supply chain, reducing the risk of counterfeiting and ensuring ethical sourcing. Additionally, blockchain enables smart contracts, automating various supply chain processes and reducing paperwork and administrative burdens.

The Internet of Things (IoT) is also playing a significant role in supply chain analytics. By connecting physical devices and sensors, retailers can collect real-time data on product location, temperature, and condition. This data can be analyzed to optimize inventory levels, streamline transportation routes, and minimize product damage. IoT devices can also be used for predictive maintenance, ensuring that equipment is serviced promptly to avoid disruptions.

Big data analytics is another critical technology that retailers should embrace. With the increasing availability of data from various sources, including social media, customer reviews, and point-of-sale systems, retailers can gain valuable insights into consumer behavior, preferences, and market trends. By harnessing big data analytics, retailers can personalize marketing campaigns, improve demand forecasting, and enhance overall customer experience.

Lastly, cloud computing offers immense benefits to retailers in terms of scalability, flexibility, and cost-effectiveness. By moving supply chain analytics to the cloud, retailers can process and store vast amounts of data without investing in expensive infrastructure. Cloud-based analytics platforms also enable collaboration and data sharing across different departments and stakeholders.

In conclusion, emerging technologies are revolutionizing supply chain analytics for retailers. AI, blockchain, IoT, big data analytics, and cloud computing are paving the way for more efficient and data-driven supply chain operations. By embracing these technologies, retailers can gain a competitive edge, optimize their supply chain processes, and ultimately improve customer satisfaction and profitability. Business standard analysts should stay updated with these emerging technologies and explore their potential applications within the retail industry.

Artificial Intelligence and Machine Learning in Retail Supply Chains

In today's rapidly evolving retail landscape, staying ahead of the competition requires retailers to embrace cutting-edge technologies that can improve efficiency and optimize operations. One such technology that has gained significant traction in recent years is Artificial Intelligence (AI) and Machine Learning (ML). By harnessing the power of AI and ML in retail supply chains, businesses can unlock a plethora of opportunities to streamline processes, enhance customer experiences, and drive profitability.

AI and ML offer immense potential for retailers to make data-driven decisions and gain valuable insights into their supply chain operations. These technologies can analyze large volumes of data from various sources, including sales data, customer behavior, inventory levels, and market trends. By leveraging this data, retailers can identify patterns, predict demand, and optimize inventory levels, ensuring products are available when and where customers need them.

One of the key applications of AI and ML in retail supply chains is demand forecasting. Traditionally, retailers relied on historical sales data and intuition to estimate future demand. However, AI and ML algorithms can analyze multiple variables, such as weather patterns, social media trends, and economic indicators, to generate accurate demand forecasts. This enables retailers to optimize inventory levels, reduce stockouts, and minimize holding costs.

Moreover, AI and ML can enhance supply chain visibility and traceability. Retailers can deploy intelligent systems that track and monitor products throughout the supply chain, ensuring transparency and minimizing the risk of counterfeit or damaged goods. These technologies can also identify potential bottlenecks or disruptions in the supply chain, allowing retailers to proactively address issues and maintain a seamless flow of goods.

Additionally, AI and ML can support personalized marketing and customer engagement. By analyzing customer data, including browsing history, purchase behavior, and preferences, retailers can deliver personalized recommendations and targeted promotions. This not only enhances the customer experience but also drives sales and customer loyalty.

As a business standard analyst in the retail industry, understanding and leveraging AI and ML in supply chain analytics is crucial for driving operational efficiency and gaining a competitive edge. By harnessing the power of these technologies, retailers can make informed decisions, optimize inventory, enhance customer experiences, and ultimately increase profitability.

In conclusion, AI and ML have emerged as game-changers in the retail sector, revolutionizing supply chain operations. By embracing these technologies, retailers can unlock valuable insights, optimize inventory levels, enhance supply chain visibility, and deliver personalized experiences to customers. As a business standard analyst, it is essential to stay informed about AI and ML advancements and explore their potential applications in retail supply chain analytics and optimization.

Big Data Analytics and its Impact on Retail Supply Chains

In today's fast-paced retail environment, where customers' expectations are higher than ever before, it is imperative for retailers to leverage the power of big data analytics to optimize their supply chain operations. By harnessing the wealth of data available to them, retailers can gain valuable insights into consumer behavior, forecasting demand, streamlining inventory management, and ultimately improving their overall operational efficiency.

The advent of big data analytics has revolutionized the way retailers approach their supply chain management. With the ability to collect and analyze vast amounts of data from various sources, such as point-of-sale systems, social media platforms, online shopping trends, and customer feedback, retailers now have a comprehensive understanding of consumer preferences and buying patterns. This valuable information enables them to make data-driven decisions that align with customer demand and optimize their supply chain operations.

One of the key benefits of big data analytics in retail supply chains is its ability to enhance demand forecasting accuracy. By analyzing historical sales data, market trends, and even external factors like weather patterns, retailers can predict future demand with a higher degree of accuracy. This allows them to optimize their inventory levels, ensuring they have the right products in the right quantities at the right locations. By avoiding stockouts and overstock situations, retailers can reduce costs, minimize waste, and improve customer satisfaction.

Additionally, big data analytics helps retailers identify areas of their supply chain that can be further optimized. By analyzing data related to transportation, warehousing, and distribution, retailers can identify bottlenecks, inefficiencies, and areas for improvement. For instance, by analyzing transportation data, retailers can optimize delivery routes, reduce transit times, and minimize fuel costs. Similarly, by analyzing warehouse data, retailers can optimize storage capacities, reduce picking errors, and improve overall operational efficiency.

Furthermore, big data analytics enables retailers to personalize the customer experience. By analyzing customer data, such as purchase history, preferences, and browsing behavior, retailers can tailor their marketing strategies and product offerings to individual customers. This level of personalization not only enhances customer satisfaction but also drives customer loyalty and repeat business.

In conclusion, big data analytics has emerged as a game-changer in the retail industry, particularly in supply chain management. By leveraging the power of data analytics, retailers can gain valuable insights into consumer behavior, optimize their supply chain operations, and ultimately improve their bottom line. As a retailer, embracing big data analytics is essential to staying competitive in today's dynamic marketplace and achieving long-term success.

Predictive Analytics for Omni-channel Retailing

In today's fast-paced retail environment, staying competitive and meeting customer demands is more challenging than ever. With the rise of omnichannel retailing, retailers need to be able to effectively manage and optimize their supply chain operations to meet the expectations of their customers across multiple channels. This is where predictive analytics comes into play, providing retailers with the insights and tools they need to make data-driven decisions and drive success in the omnichannel landscape.

Predictive analytics leverages historical data, statistical algorithms, and machine learning techniques to forecast future outcomes and trends. For retailers, this means being able to anticipate customer demand, optimize inventory levels, and improve supply chain efficiency. By analyzing data from various sources, including sales transactions, customer behavior, social media, and market trends, retailers can gain a deeper understanding of their customers and make informed decisions to meet their needs.

One of the key benefits of predictive analytics for omnichannel retailing is the ability to accurately forecast demand. By analyzing historical sales data and considering various factors such as seasonality, promotions, and customer preferences, retailers can predict future demand patterns and adjust their inventory levels accordingly. This helps retailers avoid stockouts and overstock situations, leading to improved customer satisfaction and reduced costs.

Furthermore, predictive analytics enables retailers to personalize the customer experience across multiple channels. By analyzing customer data and behavior, retailers can create targeted marketing campaigns, recommend products based on individual preferences, and provide personalized pricing and promotions. This level of personalization enhances customer engagement and loyalty, ultimately driving sales and revenue.

Business standard analysts in the retail industry play a critical role in leveraging predictive analytics for omnichannel retailing. They are responsible for gathering and analyzing data, building predictive models, and translating insights into actionable recommendations. By utilizing their expertise in data analysis and statistical modeling, business standard analysts can help retailers identify trends, optimize processes, and make strategic decisions to improve supply chain operations.

In conclusion, predictive analytics is a powerful tool for retailers operating in the omnichannel landscape. By leveraging data and advanced analytics techniques, retailers can gain a competitive edge, improve customer satisfaction, and drive business growth. Business standard analysts play a crucial role in harnessing the power of predictive analytics and translating insights into actionable strategies. Embracing predictive analytics is no longer a luxury but a necessity for retailers looking to thrive in the ever-evolving retail industry.

Chapter 8: Conclusion and Recommendations

Summary of Key Findings

In today's rapidly evolving retail industry, the need for efficient supply chain management has become more critical than ever. As a retailer, understanding and leveraging supply chain analytics and optimization techniques can give you a competitive edge in the market. This subchapter provides a concise summary of the key findings from the book "The Retailer's Guide to Supply Chain Analytics and Optimization," tailored to meet the needs of retailers and business standard analysts.

1. Importance of Supply Chain Analytics: The book emphasizes the significance of supply chain analytics in driving profitability and customer satisfaction. By harnessing the power of data and advanced analytical techniques, retailers can gain valuable insights into various aspects of their supply chain, such as demand forecasting, inventory management, and transportation optimization.

2. Demand Forecasting: Accurate demand forecasting is crucial for retailers to optimize inventory levels and ensure product availability. The book explores different forecasting methods and highlights the benefits of leveraging historical data, market trends, and customer behavior analysis to predict demand more accurately.

3. Inventory Optimization: Efficient inventory management is a key driver of profitability. The book provides insights into how retailers can leverage analytics to optimize their inventory levels, reduce carrying costs, and minimize stockouts. Techniques such as ABC

analysis, safety stock calculations, and economic order quantity (EOQ) models are discussed in detail.

4. Supplier Collaboration: Building strong relationships with suppliers is essential for smooth supply chain operations. The book emphasizes the importance of leveraging analytics to improve supplier collaboration, negotiate better terms, and enhance overall supply chain efficiency.

5. Transportation Optimization: The transportation aspect of the supply chain plays a crucial role in ensuring timely and cost-effective delivery. The book explores different optimization techniques, including route optimization, carrier selection, and load consolidation, to help retailers streamline their transportation operations and reduce costs.

6. Technology and Tools: The subchapter highlights various technologies and tools available to retailers for supply chain analytics and optimization. It covers topics such as data management systems, predictive analytics software, and real-time tracking technologies, providing retailers with a comprehensive understanding of the options available to them.

By embracing supply chain analytics and optimization techniques highlighted in this book, retailers can enhance operational efficiency, reduce costs, and deliver an exceptional customer experience. Whether you are a retailer or a business standard analyst, the key findings summarized in this subchapter will equip you with the knowledge and insights necessary to thrive in the fast-paced world of retail supply chain management.

Recommendations for Retailers Implementing Supply Chain Analytics

In today's highly competitive retail landscape, supply chain analytics has become an indispensable tool for retailers looking to optimize their operations and gain a competitive edge. By harnessing the power of data and analytics, retailers can make more informed decisions, streamline their supply chain processes, and enhance overall operational efficiency. This subchapter provides a comprehensive set of recommendations for retailers aiming to implement supply chain analytics successfully.

1. Establish Clear Objectives: Before diving into supply chain analytics, it is crucial for retailers to define their goals and objectives. Whether it's reducing costs, improving customer satisfaction, or enhancing inventory management, having a clear vision will help guide the implementation process effectively.

2. Invest in the Right Technology: To leverage the full potential of supply chain analytics, retailers must invest in the appropriate technology infrastructure. This includes robust data management systems, advanced analytics tools, and cloud-based platforms for real-time data access and collaboration.

3. Build a Cross-Functional Team: Implementing supply chain analytics requires collaboration across different departments. Retailers should form a cross-functional team comprising business standard analysts, IT specialists, supply chain managers, and other key stakeholders. This team will ensure seamless integration of analytics into the existing supply chain processes.

4. Collect and Cleanse Relevant Data: High-quality data is the foundation of effective supply chain analytics. Retailers should identify the key data points required for analysis and establish processes to collect, cleanse, and store this data accurately. This may involve integrating data from various sources, such as point-of-sale systems, inventory management systems, and customer relationship management platforms.

5. Leverage Predictive Analytics: Predictive analytics can provide valuable insights into future demand patterns, allowing retailers to optimize inventory levels, improve forecasting accuracy, and enhance supply chain responsiveness. Retailers should invest in predictive modeling techniques and leverage historical data to identify trends and patterns.

6. Monitor Key Performance Indicators: Implementing supply chain analytics is an ongoing process. Retailers should identify and track key performance indicators (KPIs) to measure the effectiveness of their supply chain operations continuously. These KPIs may include on-time delivery rates, order accuracy, inventory turnover, and customer satisfaction.

7. Foster a Data-Driven Culture: To truly benefit from supply chain analytics, retailers must foster a data-driven culture within their organization. This involves training employees on data analysis techniques, encouraging data-driven decision-making, and providing access to analytics tools and insights.

By following these recommendations, retailers can unlock the full potential of supply chain analytics and optimize their operations for success in today's dynamic retail environment. Embracing data-driven decision-making and leveraging advanced analytics techniques will undoubtedly enable retailers to stay ahead of the competition, enhance customer experience, and drive business growth.

Future Outlook for Supply Chain Analytics in Retail

In today's fast-paced retail industry, data-driven decision-making is crucial for success. As a retailer, understanding and optimizing your supply chain is essential to improving operational efficiency, reducing costs, and enhancing customer satisfaction. To help you navigate through the complex world of supply chain analytics, this appendix provides a collection of sample models and templates that you can use as a starting point for your own analysis.

1. Demand Forecasting Model: Accurate demand forecasting is the cornerstone of effective supply chain management. This template offers a step-by-step guide on how to develop a demand forecasting model using historical sales data, market trends, and other relevant factors. By leveraging this model, you can optimize inventory levels, minimize stockouts, and improve customer service.

2. Inventory Optimization Model: Excessive inventory levels tie up capital and increase carrying costs, while insufficient inventory leads to stockouts and lost sales opportunities. This template illustrates different inventory optimization techniques, such as Economic Order Quantity (EOQ) and Just-In-Time (JIT), to help you strike the right balance between inventory costs and service levels.

3. Supplier Performance Dashboard: Monitoring supplier performance is crucial for maintaining a reliable supply chain. This model provides a comprehensive dashboard that tracks key supplier metrics, such as on-time delivery, quality, and cost. By identifying underperforming suppliers, you can initiate corrective actions, negotiate better terms, or explore alternative sourcing options.

4. Transportation Optimization Model: Efficient transportation management is critical for delivering products to customers on time and at the lowest cost. This template outlines various transportation optimization algorithms, such as the Vehicle Routing Problem (VRP) and the Traveling Salesman Problem (TSP). By applying these models, you can optimize route planning, consolidate shipments, and reduce transportation costs.

5. Network Design Model: As your retail business evolves, so should your supply chain network. This model provides a framework for evaluating different network design scenarios, such as the number and location of warehouses or distribution centers. By analyzing factors like customer demand patterns, transportation costs, and facility capacities, you can optimize your supply chain network for maximum efficiency and responsiveness.

These sample supply chain analytics models and templates are designed to assist business standard analysts in the retail industry. They offer a starting point for retailers to leverage data and analytics to optimize their supply chain operations. By using these models, retailers can make informed decisions, improve operational efficiency, reduce costs, and enhance customer satisfaction. Embracing supply chain analytics is no longer an option but a necessity for retailers looking to thrive in today's competitive market.

www.ingramcontent.com/pod-product-compliance
Lightning Source LLC
LaVergne TN
LVHW052002060526
838201LV00059B/3783